Fabulous and Monstrous Beasts

Belinda Weber

KINGFISHER
NEW YORK

Consultant: Neil Philip

Copyright © 2008 by Macmillan Children's Books
KINGFISHER
Published in the United States by Kingfisher, an imprint of Henry Holt
and Company LLC, 175 Fifth Avenue, New York, New York 10010.
First published in Great Britain by Kingfisher Publications plc, an imprint
of Macmillan Children's Books, London.

Distributed in Canada by H. B. Fenn and Company Ltd.

Library of Congress Cataloging-in-Publication Data
Weber, Belinda.
Fabulous and monstrous beasts / Belinda Weber.—1st American ed.
p. cm.
Includes index.
ISBN 978-0-7534-6247-8
1. Animals, Mythical—Juvenile literature. 2. Monsters—Juvenile
literature. I. Title.
GR825.W38 2008
398.24'54—dc22
2007047765

ISBN: 978-0-7534-6247-8

Kingfisher books are available for special promotions and premiums.
For details contact: Director of Special Markets, Holtzbrinck Publishers.

First American Edition October 2008
Printed in China
1 3 5 7 9 10 8 6 4 2
1TR/0508/GC/UTDG/140GSM/F

NOTE TO READERS
The website addresses listed in this book are correct at the time of
going to print. However, due to the ever-changing nature of the Internet,
website addresses and content can change. Websites can contain links
that are unsuitable for children. The publisher cannot be held responsible
for changes in website addresses or content or for information
obtained through third-party websites. We strongly advise that
Internet searches are supervised by an adult.

CONTENTS

CREATURES OF THE AIR

The natural world is not always easy to understand. Powerful storms, floods, droughts, or other terrible events can devastate entire areas and kill hundreds of people. Since ancient times, people have told stories about gods and monsters to help make sense of these catastrophes. By adding a dash of imagination to known facts about living animals, people conjured up fabulous beasts that were capable of wreaking havoc. Dragons, in particular, were associated with the weather. When angered, they might bring about thunderstorms and rain—or they might hold back water to cause a drought.

Lightning strikes
Many ancient peoples thought that lightning was a sign of the gods' anger. The Norse god of storms, Thor, was said to throw lightning bolts at his enemies.

Flying through the sky

Winged creatures often appear in ancient stories. The Greeks explained the cycle of day and night with their tale of the god Helios, who carried the sun across the sky in a chariot that was pulled by four white horses with winged feet. Daylight shone from the horses' manes and flames flickered from their nostrils. In India, there is a belief that elephants used to be able to fly. The Moklum people, who live along India's border with Myanmar (formerly Burma), tell how the creator, Rang, made an elephant with wings, but whenever the heavy creature landed, it broke trees and destroyed crops. So Rang took away its wings and gave it legs made out of plantains, a type of banana.

God of thunder

In Japanese mythology, dragons were gods of thunder and lightning. Their breath changed into clouds that could produce rain or fire. Despite their terrible power, these dragons were welcomed because they brought people wealth and fortune.

Dragons

Violent storms were often blamed on dragons. In some cultures, thunder and lightning were said to be caused by dragons fighting in the sky, while floods happened when dragons fought in the water. In Japan, dragons protected rivers and lakes and were seen as gods. In times of drought, people tried to wake up dragons, which were said to sleep at the bottoms of lakes or rivers. Once awake, the angry dragons might fly up into the skies and cause rain.

Vietnamese dragons
Vietnamese dragons, like Chinese ones, represent fertility, life, and growth. The ones on this piece of furniture are guarding the circular yin and yang symbol, which stands for all the energy in the universe. Eastern rulers used dragons to represent their power.

Dangerous creatures

Western dragons were much more dangerous than Eastern ones. They often demanded human sacrifices to stop them from causing havoc. They held people prisoner, too, and hoarded treasures inside their dens. Dragons from Western lands were often hunted and killed, either for their gold or to free the hostages they held. Saint George is the most famous dragon slayer. Legend tells how George traveled to a town in Libya where a terrible dragon had made its nest beside a spring. It terrorized the local people whenever they came to get water and demanded that a young girl be sacrificed each day. On the day that George passed the spring, the king's daughter, Sabra, had been tied up and left for the dragon to eat. Brave Saint George killed the dragon and rescued the princess.

Chinese New Year
The dragon dance is one of the highlights of Chinese New Year celebrations and is said to bring good luck. Dancers move a dragon puppet to mimic the flow of a river.

Strength and fury

A wyvern, or *vouivre*, was a type of flying serpent with eagle's wings, two legs, and a tail that ended in a sharp barb. It usually lived alone in its lair, which was piled high with bones and trinkets. Wyverns were not as clever as dragons and could be fooled by shiny things—so not all of their treasures were gold. Even so, they fought hard to protect their stash, using their beaklike jaws and sharp talons. The wyvern sometimes appears on coats of arms as a symbol of strength and fury.

Slaying the dragon

Western dragons were evil, bloodthirsty monsters that could breathe fire. Only the very bravest knights dared fight one. In many legends, a knight who killed a dragon won the hand of a princess in marriage.

Pegasus

In Greek mythology, Pegasus was a gentle winged horse that sprang from the blood of a monster named Medusa. The hero Bellerophon tried to take Pegasus to the gods' home, Mount Olympus, but the gods sent a gadfly to sting Pegasus so that he threw off his rider (see page 23). Then Pegasus was welcomed into the sky, where he became a constellation, or pattern of stars.

Magical horses

Valued for their grace, beauty, strength, and speed, horses have been used for transportation for thousands of years. Farmers sometimes used workhorses to pull their carts and plows. Sleek and speedy thoroughbreds, which only the rich could afford, were symbols of power and wealth. Ancient kings were often buried with horses to use as transportation in the afterworld. Mythical horses were even stronger and more powerful than real ones. Some had wings or extra legs. Stories of magical horses helped explain how the sun moved across the sky or how the gods traveled vast distances.

Collecting the souls of the dead

The Valkyries were female warriors from Norse myths who lived with Odin in the hall of Valhalla. In times of war, they rode their horses through the battlefields deciding which warriors would find victory or defeat. They carried off the victorious dead to live with them in Valhalla.

The fastest mount in the world

In Norse mythology, the chief god, Odin, rode Sleipnir, a horse with eight legs. Sleipnir was the offspring of Loki, the trickster god, and Svadilfari, a stallion that belonged to a giant. Loki had changed himself into a beautiful mare in order to lure Svadilfari away from his owner. Months later, when Loki returned to the gods, he was leading Sleipnir, the eight-legged foal that Svadilfari had fathered. Sleipnir was so fast that he could outrun anything. He could also carry Odin down to the land of the dead.

Odin's horse

The name of Odin's horse, Sleipnir, means "gliding one" in the Norse language and is related to the English word *slippery*. Sleipnir was so fast that he was able to gallop over land and sea and through the air. When he and his master, Odin, who was the god of war, rode into battle, they were sometimes flanked by a pair of wild wolves.

Son of the sun god

One day the Greek sun god allowed his son, Phaëthon, to drive his chariot and carry the sun across the sky. However, Phaëthon could not control the horses. The sun came too close to the earth and scorched its surface. To stop the land from being destroyed by fire, Zeus struck down the boy with a thunderbolt.

Immortal birds

Death is very hard to understand, and people have stories that help them come to terms with it. In many different cultures, people believe in some kind of afterworld where souls continue living after death. Birds are often associated with ideas of immortality. In Christianity, the hatching of a chick from its egg is a symbol of rebirth, used to celebrate the resurrection of Jesus Christ at Easter. Some legends tell of birds that could complete one life cycle and then bring themselves back to life again, whereas other mythical birds had life spans of billions of years. Because of their age, these creatures were thought to have great wisdom, so their advice was sought by both kings and commoners.

Glowing feathers
In Russian folklore, the firebird was a beautiful bird whose feathers glowed red, orange, and yellow. Just one feather from its tail was enough to light up a room. The firebird gave hope to the needy and even dripped pearls from its beak—but it also brought doom to anyone who captured it.

Reborn through fire
The phoenix was a bird that could resurrect itself after death and begin its life all over again. After living for 500 years, the phoenix knew that it was time to die and built a nest made out of cassia and frankincense sticks. There it sat, singing a beautiful song, as the sun set fire to the nest. Both bird and nest were destroyed by the flames, but a worm crawled from the ashes and developed into a new phoenix. This idea of rebirth was a great comfort to many people and helped them understand the concepts of life and death.

Birth of a phoenix

After its rebirth, the new phoenix collected the ashes and put them inside an egg made of myrrh. It carried the egg to Egypt and buried it in a temple. Then the phoenix returned to Arabia, ready to begin its life anew.

Wise old bird

The simurgh is a bird from Persian mythology. Its name means "like 30 birds" and is a tribute to its size and power. The simurgh is so old that it has seen the universe destroyed three times. It lives in the tree of knowledge and possesses the wisdom of ages. It spreads knowledge by blowing seeds from the tree all around the world. Its flapping wings sound like thunder, and one touch from a wing can heal any wound.

The Chinese phoenix

Unlike the ordinary phoenix, the Chinese phoenix, or *feng-hwang*, lived with a partner, and both birds sang beautiful, joyful songs. Images of these birds are often used as wedding decorations, symbolizing a perfect union. The name *feng-hwang* is made up of the words for the male bird (*feng*) and the female (*hwang*).

Giant birds

In many cultures, birds were associated with the weather. The bigger the bird, the more dramatic the weather conditions that it controlled. As bringers of floods and storms, birds such as the North American thunderbird were very feared. Knowing what angered or delighted them could mean the difference between a life-giving rain shower and a destructive deluge. Other huge birds guarded precious treasures or possessed great strength. Garuda, a giant bird from Hindu mythology, represented life itself. Whatever their special attributes were, all monster birds had to be kept happy so that they did not cause disasters.

Thunder and rain

Native Americans believed that their storm spirit, the thunderbird, could create thunder by flapping its wings and could also shoot bolts of lightning from its eyes. They painted images of the thunderbird on tepees and carved totem poles in its shape. They believed that the thunderbird protected them from evil spirits.

Bird food

The roc appears in Arabian fairy tales. It was an enormous bird of prey with a 50-ft. (15-m) wingspan, and it laid eggs that were taller than humans! The roc was thought to prey on baby elephants. It would lift one up into the air and then drop it so that it smashed on the rocks below. Then the roc swooped down and feasted on the remains of the calf at its leisure. The North American thunderbird, which was strong enough to rip apart trees, was also said to carry off animals. Unlike the roc, it could bring good fortune if its spirit appeared to people in dreams.

Sinbad and the roc

1001 Nights, a collection of stories that dates back to around A.D. 850, includes the adventures of a sailor named Sinbad. On his fifth voyage, his shipmates find a roc's egg on a desert island and eat the chick inside. Soon the angry roc parent catches up with the ship and pelts it with boulders until it sinks. Here, Sinbad is battling with the roc.

Bird of life

In Hindu myths, Garuda is the enormous king of the birds, part eagle and part human. Here he is carrying the god Vishnu and his wife, Lakshmi. As well as being the bird of life, Garuda is a destroyer, feared by snakes and dragons. In Indonesia, people thought that a picture of Garuda could wake up a sleeping dragon so that it brought life-giving rain.

Guarding treasures

With the head and wings of an eagle and the body of a lion, the griffin was a formidable beast. In Indian myths, it dug gold from the mountains to make its nests and collected agate, a gem, to protect its young from sickness. Anyone foolish enough to try to steal a griffin's treasure was fed to its young. Medieval kings and nobles often drank from cups carved from griffins' claws, though the cups were actually made from antelope horns. They believed that the claws changed color in the presence of poison.

13

Harpies and Gorgons

Many fearsome monsters combine human and animal features. The Harpies of ancient Greek mythology had women's heads but the bodies and wings of eagles or vultures. Sometimes known as the "snatchers," Harpies would steal people with their long talons and torment them in the underworld. They were said to appear in storms and whirlwinds and always left a foul stench behind. Even today, people use the word *harpy* to describe a greedy, annoying woman.

Explaining greed and anger

Mixing human and animal characteristics might have helped people understand the more selfish sides of their natures. Emotions such as greed, jealousy, and anger can lead people to wish or do horrible things—which were possibly easier to imagine or explain as acts of vengeance by a monster. Gorgons illustrated the power of anger, for example, as they could turn someone to stone with only one glance. Today the word *gorgon* can be used to describe a woman with a fiery temper. In ancient times, images of Gorgons' heads were often placed on doors, coins, or armor to ward off evil spirits.

Hissing hair
Gorgons were recognized by their hair, which was a writhing mass of snakes. The goddess Athena had been so jealous of the Gorgon Medusa's fair locks that she had them changed to serpents! Gorgons also had golden wings.

The avengers

This painting shows two of the three Furies, spirits from Roman mythology who sought revenge for people who had been wronged. These women were sometimes shown with the wings of a bat or bird, with serpent hair, or with the head or body of a dog.

Tormenting travelers

Harpies were among the most dangerous creatures of the underworld. No one knew how many there were, but these robbers came with the storm winds and kidnapped people or took their food. Harpies often appear on ancient Greek monuments as symbols of death. Only one thing could scare away a harpy—the sound of a brass instrument.

Vampires

Vampires are creatures of nightmares. These shape-shifting beings live by sucking the blood of others. Seemingly dead by day, vampires shun daylight—and may even crumble to dust in the sun's rays. As night falls, however, they rise up, usually in the form of a bat or a human, and hunt down their next victim. One bite from a vampire not only takes away a person's life, but it also turns him or her into a vampire!

Force for good

Real-life vampire bats feed on the blood of other mammals, usually cattle. So that they can feed without their victims' wounds scabbing over, the bats' saliva contains a substance that stops blood from clotting. This substance is now being used in a medicine to help fight strokes and other conditions caused by blood clots.

Out for the count

Written in 1897, Bram Stoker's *Dracula* told of a well-mannered count who changed into a vampire each evening. Dracula's thirst for blood captured the imagination of readers and filmmakers. His story has been made into many movies, including *Horror of Dracula* (1958), shown below, starring Christopher Lee.

A global phenomenon

There are stories of vampires from all around the world, including China, Arabia, and the Americas, but they are most associated with Eastern Europe. In many places, the vampire assumes the shape of another animal, such as a wolf or a dog, but in some stories the vampire appears as mist or smoke. Many charms are used to keep vampires away, including garlic, holy water, hawthorn sprigs, or mustard seeds.

Killer kitty

The most notorious Japanese vampire was the two-tailed cat of Nabeshima, which strangled a princess. The cat took the shape of the princess and bewitched a prince so that his strength slowly faded away. Only the courage of a brave and faithful soldier thwarted the vampire's plans. The evil cat escaped to the mountains but was hunted down and killed.

Grave fears

Cemeteries were feared, especially at night, because a vampire might rise up from one of the graves. It was thought, however, that a sure-footed white stallion that had never mated could tell which graves housed vampires. This type of horse would be led through a graveyard to see if it refused to walk over any of the graves—a sure sign that a grave contained a vampire.

CREATURES OF THE LAND

Planet Earth is subject to powerful natural forces. Earthquakes tear gaping holes in the ground. Erupting volcanoes hurl fire, rocks, and burning lava up into the sky. Like destructive weather, people explained these events by associating them with gods, monsters, and other mythological beings. Earthquakes, for example, could be caused by the foot stamping of an angry giant. Many monsters were at least partly human. Others, such as the fire-breathing Chimera or the many-headed Hydra, borrowed elements from ordinary animals but had monstrous powers.

Fiery forge

The ancient Romans believed that the volcano Etna was home to Vulcan, the god of fire. They thought that the flames and ash they could see were created as Vulcan crafted thunderbolts, tools, and weapons for the other gods.

Safe harvest

When people learned to farm the land, they turned to the gods to help them do so. A bad harvest could leave people hungry and vulnerable to illnesses. In ancient Rome, people thanked Ceres, the goddess of farming, by holding a harvest feast when they had gathered the crops. In European folklore, brownies often lived on farms. They helped farmers care for their animals but would play mean tricks if they were not thanked with gifts of cakes or bowls of milk.

Farming Fenoderee

Fenoderee was a fairy that lived on the Isle of Man in the Irish Sea. He was very strong and helped farmers gather the harvest, but he was also offended easily—if that happened, the farmer had to fend for himself.

Unicorns

One of the most beautiful fantasy creatures, the unicorn was an elegant white horse with a spiral horn on its forehead. Known for its loud bellowing, it was very fierce—but became meek and mild in the presence of an innocent young woman. In Christian imagery, a unicorn and a maiden represented Christ and his mother, Mary. But long before its association with Christ, the unicorn was a symbol of goodness, innocence, and purity.

Enchanted by a maiden

Capturing a unicorn was a tricky business, as the animals were wild and could be aggressive. Only a young girl could quiet the creature. Upon seeing her, the unicorn would settle down to sleep with its head in her lap. Hunters pursued unicorns for their precious horns. They would use a maiden to lure and trap their prey and then move in when the animal was asleep.

Real unicorns?

Through the years, many people have claimed to own unicorn horns. In most cases, the horn was probably the spiral tusk of a narwhal, a member of the whale family that lives in the Arctic Ocean. Its tusk can grow to as long as 10 ft. (3m). Vikings and other traders, knowing about the unicorn myth, might have sold these tusks as unicorn horns for many times their weight in gold. Sometimes the tusks were carved into goblets to protect the drinkers from swallowing poison.

Special powers

Unicorn horns were thought to be magical. Many rich and powerful people claimed to have captured a unicorn and taken its horn in order to gain access to its magic. Like a griffin's claws (see page 13), a unicorn's horn could detect poison—just a single touch was said to be enough to reveal any life-threatening ingredients. Even better, the horn could remove the poison, making the food or water safe again. Dust filed from a unicorn's horn could purify water. It was sometimes sprinkled down wells to clean the water inside them.

The lion and the unicorn

When King James VI of Scotland succeeded Elizabeth I of England in 1603, he designed a new royal insignia. He placed one of the unicorns from the Scottish coat of arms near the lion of the English coat of arms and showed them both supporting a shield. The insignia was supposed to symbolize how the Scots and English would be united from then on.

Eastern unicorns

This embroidered silk badge shows a *ki-lin*, or Chinese unicorn. In Eastern mythology, a unicorn had a long horn, the body of a deer, and the hooves of a horse. The *kirin*, or Japanese unicorn, was very similar in appearance to the *ki-lin*, but it was covered in scales. Eastern unicorns were gentle, peaceful creatures that brought good luck. They picked their way through grass very carefully so that they would not harm any insects on the ground.

The Chimera

Many mythical beasts were so dangerous that they did not need to attack using claws or teeth; they could breathe fire, spit poison—or both! The Chimera of Greek mythology was a fire-breathing monster with the front legs of a lion, the body of a goat, and a serpent's tail. She symbolized death and destruction and came from a monstrous family. Her parents were Echidna, the goddess of sickness and disease, and Typhon, the god of winter storms. Her siblings included Cerberus, the hound of Hades, and the nine-headed Hydra.

Snarling Chimera
In this sculpture made in 1947 by Italian artist Arturo Martini, the Chimera has become a male. It does not have a goat's body, but its tail does look like a serpent's. There are many different interpretations of the Chimera, all of them fearsome.

Three heads are better than one
The Chimera is usually shown with three heads—a lion's, a goat's, and a serpent's. In some sources the goat breathes fire, but here, flames burst from the lion's mouth. Most versions of the story agree that the Chimera could run extremely fast, so she must have had muscular legs. Her speed and incredible power made her a formidable enemy.

Fearful ride

This 17th-century French pitcher shows the Chimera being ridden by cherubs. The wavy blue background might represent the ocean. The Chimera was associated with storms, shipwrecks, and—because of her ability to breathe fire—volcanoes, too.

The rise and fall of Bellerophon

According to Greek legends, the Chimera was killed by the hero Bellerophon. King Iobates of Lycia was asked by his son-in-law to have Bellerophon killed—but instead, the king gave Bellerophon the task of killing the Chimera, which was terrorizing his kingdom. Following his victory over the monster, Bellerophon became too proud. He tried to ride Pegasus to Mount Olympus (see page 8), where mortals were forbidden. Zeus, the king of the gods, was so enraged by his arrogance that he stripped him of his glory. Poor Bellerophon died a beggar.

Death of the Chimera

Riding the winged horse Pegasus, Bellerophon rained arrows down on the Chimera. Then the young prince used his spear to thrust a lump of metal between her jaws. When the Chimera tried to breathe fire at her attacker, the lead melted and choked her to death.

Scales and feathers

Mythical creatures had various ways of killing their victims. Some were armed with sharp talons and teeth. Others could give fatal glances that killed a person on the spot. The basilisk was a deadly creature that had more ways of attacking than most. With the head and body of a rooster and a serpent's tail, the basilisk spat venom and could kill with just one look. It destroyed every living thing—animal or plant—that it came near. If it drank from a well, the water remained polluted for hundreds of years. One way to kill a basilisk was with a mirror. The sight of its own reflection made it die of fright!

The cockatrice
In legends from the Middle Ages, a new form of the basilisk appeared—the cockatrice. This four-legged rooster had long, thorny wings and a snakelike tail that ended in a hook.

The bird serpent

Many different peoples in Central America, including the Mixtec, Toltec, and Aztecs, believed in a creator god who was part bird and part serpent. They called this god Quetzalcoatl, from *quetzal* (a colorful tropical bird with a long tail) and *coatl* (their word for *serpent*). The god was also known as the Feathered Serpent. Quetzalcoatl was believed to be life and death, light and dark, and heaven and earth all at once. The Toltec told how he had traveled to the underworld to collect some bones and then sprinkled them with his blood to create the first humans. Quetzalcoatl taught people how to farm, weave, make calendars, and understand the movements of the stars.

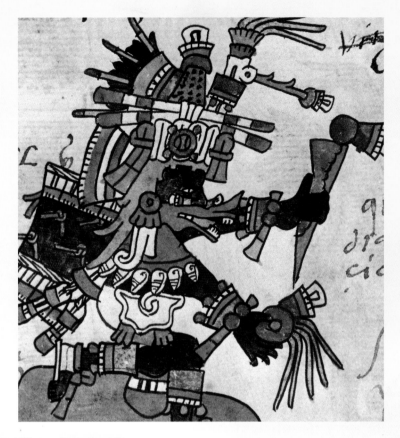

Strange family

People thought that basilisks hatched from eggs that had been laid by roosters, possibly on a dung hill, and kept warm by a snake or toad. In some descriptions, they had fiery breath and, in others, a terrifying roar.

Picturing a god

This image of Quetzalcoatl is from a 16th-century Aztec codex, or book. In Toltec imagery, the god sometimes wears a white mask. Some historians think that Spanish General Hernando Cortés was able to conquer the Aztecs because they mistook him for the god Quetzalcoatl.

Serpents and salamanders

Snakes are powerful creatures in myths, able to protect or destroy. The Dahomey people of western Africa believed that a rainbow serpent called Aido Hwedo supported the planet on its coils. Earthquakes happened when Aido Hwedo grew uncomfortable and shifted his position. In Hindu mythology, a snake is also responsible for earthquakes. When the world serpent, Sesha, shakes one of his thousand heads, the land trembles.

Kind or cruel?

Snakes were also associated with water. The nagas of Indian myths were snake gods whose kings lived in beautiful underwater palaces. Nagas controlled the rain and protected pools, lakes, and rivers. They could be dangerous or generous, depending on their moods. Other snakes, including the Hydra, were always hostile. The Hydra, a sibling of the Chimera, lived in a swamp and preyed on cattle. Its poisonous breath destroyed crops and any people it touched.

Protecting Buddha
Calmed by Buddha's gentle teachings, this naga coils its body into a seat and shelters Buddha with its hooded head. In India, statues of nagas are placed under trees and the space around them is left to grow wild as a haven for snakes.

Fire lizard
In medieval folklore, salamanders were said to be born in glass-blowers' furnaces and live in fires. The stories were probably based on the fire salamander, a European amphibian that hibernates inside logs. People might have collected logs for their fires and then seen salamanders in the flames, trying to escape.

Horrible Hydra

The hero Hercules was sent to kill the nine-headed Hydra—but each time he cut off one head, two more grew in its place. Eventually, Hercules's nephew helped by sealing each stump with a burning branch, and at last the monster was defeated.

Hooves and horns

Folklore is rich with stories of creatures that are half human, half beast. They have the benefit of human qualities, such as wisdom and compassion, as well as an animal's physical power. In Greek mythology, centaurs were part man and part horse. Chiron, the most famous centaur, was known for his wisdom and patience. Satyrs, also from Greek mythology, and fauns, their Roman counterparts, had horned heads with human faces and small upturned noses, human torsos, and goat legs. They loved music and dancing.

Gentle teacher

Many of the centaurs were wild and enjoyed drinking too much, but Chiron was gentle and kind. He taught the gods healing arts. Although Chiron was immortal, he was wounded by a poisoned arrow. He gave away his immortality rather than live forever in pain. The god Zeus created the constellation Sagittarius in memory of him.

Music for the Satyrs

The Greek god Pan was the leader of the Satyrs. A shepherd, Pan spent his days on the hillsides, where he played a seven-reed pipe—an instrument that is known, in his honor, as the panpipes. Pan was usually friendly, unless he was woken up. If anyone was foolish enough to wake him, Pan would fly into a rage and plague the creature with nightmares.

Keeping guard

In ancient Mesopotamia, lamassus were kind protectors who represented strength and wisdom. They had human heads and the bodies of a winged bull or a lion. Many houses and palaces had lamassus carved above their doors, where they would watch over the household. This lamassu statue is one of a pair that guarded the gates of the palace of Emperor Sargon II, who lived during the 700s B.C.

Bull-headed monster

The Minotaur was a ferocious man-eater that had a bull's head and the body of a man. It was kept by King Minos of Crete in a labyrinth, or maze. Every nine years, the king demanded seven boys and seven girls from Athens, which he had defeated in battle. He sent the youngsters into the labyrinth where, confused by the puzzle of paths, they were doomed to be devoured by the Minotaur. Theseus, the prince of Athens, volunteered to be chosen for the sacrifice so that he could kill the Minotaur. He was helped by Ariadne, the daughter of King Minos, who had fallen in love with him.

Following a thread

Ariadne gave Theseus a sword and a ball of thread. She told him to unravel the thread as he moved through the labyrinth so that he would be able to find his way out again. Theseus killed the Minotaur with the sword and emerged from the labyrinth a hero.

The mysterious Sphinx

The Sphinx was a mythological creature that first appeared in ancient Egypt, where its statue guarded temples and tombs. Egyptian Sphinxes always had the body of a lion, but the head could be that of a human, a ram, or a hawk. Later the Greeks added the Sphinx to their own mythology but said that it lived in Thebes, Egypt. The Greek Sphinx was usually shown with the head of a woman, the body of a lion, and the wings of an eagle. Its parents were Echidna and Typhon, whose other offspring included the Hydra.

Giant Sphinx
One of the world's largest and oldest statues, the Great Sphinx of Giza, Egypt, was sculpted from limestone around 4,500 years ago. It has a lion's body and a man's head. It stands beside the three pyramids of Giza, which were built for the pharaohs Khufu (Cheops), Khafra, and Menkaura.

A riddle or your life
The Greek Sphinx devoured passing travelers if they could not answer this riddle: "What walks on all fours in the morning, on two feet at noon, and on three in the evening?" Oedipus was the first person to solve the puzzle. The answer was a human, who crawls on all fours as a baby, stands on two feet as an adult, but leans on a cane in old age. Furious that someone had figured out the riddle, the Sphinx smashed itself against the rocks, and Oedipus was declared the king of Thebes.

Protective spirits

Asian Sphinxes were powerful creatures that could ward off evil and wash away sins. In southern India, Sphinxes known as *purushamrigas* were carved into temple gateways and entrances in order to protect devotees as they came to worship. Thai Sphinxes had human heads and upper bodies and the lower bodies of a lion or deer, but they walked upright on two legs. They were usually found in pairs and protected people. Burmese legends tell how Buddhist monks created their Sphinx, known as *manusiha*, to prevent a royal baby from being eaten by an ogress.

Transporting gods

This Indian Sphinx stands in a temple in Chidambaram, southern India. *Purushamriga* means "human beast." As well as being guardian statues, some *purushamrigas* are used to carry statues of temple gods during religious processions and celebrations.

Goblins, hobgoblins, and fairies

Sometimes known as "little people," goblins, hobgoblins, and fairies were usually friendly but could also be spiteful. Some helped with the housework or harvests. Others jumped out at people to scare them and made milk and cream curdle. Parents who wanted their children to behave might mention the bugaboo or bugbear. Ink black in color and shifting in shape, this shadowy creature slipped down chimneys at night to kidnap naughty children. In some versions of the story, the creature took the shape of a bear and gobbled up children who had wandered too far from their parents while walking outside.

Kobolds

German folklore features little people called kobolds. The most common types were like house elves and lived alongside humans in their homes. Depending on their moods, they might tackle household chores—or play nasty tricks. Other kobolds lived in forests or under the ground in mines and mountains.

Noisy bogles

In Celtic mythology, bogles were small goblins that lived in people's houses. If the bogles were well cared for, they would help out around the house. But if they got angry, they would wait until nighttime and then bang all the pots and pans together, making so much noise that no one could fall asleep!

Lutins

In this painting, *lutins* dance around a fire next to some standing stones in northern France. *Lutins* are types of hobgoblins. Sometimes they turn into a horse, tempt someone to mount, and then throw the rider into a ditch. *Lutins* also appear as spiders, gusts of wind, flames, small boys, or monks in red habits.

Bogeymen

Called *boggelmen* in Germany, *bubak* in Bohemia, and *bodaich* in Scotland, bogeymen are known all around the world. They have no fixed form—they are the scary creatures that lurk in dark places. Children, in particular, fear bogeymen hiding under their beds or inside their closets. Fortunately, these evil spirits are not very smart, so they can be outwitted easily. In some Irish stories, bogeymen were fairies that lived in bogs and kidnapped children. They did not harm the children—they just played with them for a year and a day before returning them to their parents.

33

Bigfoot and abominable snowmen

Snow-covered mountains, dense forests, and other remote places are often so inhospitable that few people live or even go there. This makes it possible to imagine that these places could be inhabited by strange creatures who choose to stay far away from humans. The Himalaya Mountains of Nepal and Tibet are said to be home to a massive apelike creature known as the abominable snowman or yeti. Many people claim to have found snowman footprints in the snow, and some mountaineers even say that they have heard the snowman's yelping cry. A similar beast, known as Bigfoot or Sasquatch, is believed to roam the remote forests of the northwestern United States and western Canada.

Missing evidence
This hand and piece of scalp, on display at a Buddhist monastery in Pangboche, near Mount Everest in Nepal, were said to be from an abominable snowman. The hand was stolen in the 1990s.

Caught on camera
In 1967, Americans Roger Patterson and Robert Gimlin filmed an apelike creature walking through a forest in northern California. They claimed it was Bigfoot, but some said that it was a man in an ape costume. However, the footage clearly shows the creature's shoulder and thigh muscles moving, and this effect would be hard to produce in a costume.

Great apes

Both the abominable snowman and Bigfoot are said to be much larger than a human being, possibly as tall as 10 ft. (3m), and covered in reddish brown hair. The first written reference to the abominable snowman dates back to 1832, but the legend is undoubtedly older. Similarly, British explorer David Thompson reported seeing Bigfoot in 1811, but the creature was known to Native Americans much earlier. According to eyewitnesses, Bigfoot is still alive and well. In December 2006, a search party investigating a sighting in Saskatchewan, Canada, found 23-in. (60-cm)-long footprints and a tuft of fur.

Yeti in the snow
Sightings of yetis are extremely rare. In the 1920s, a Greek photographer visiting the Himalayas saw a large hairy figure in the distance. It was pulling up shrubs, apparently looking for food to eat.

Snowman footprint
This photograph, the first of an abominable snowman footprint, was taken on Mount Everest in 1951 by British explorers Eric Shipton and Michael Ward. They discovered almost 1 mi. (1.5km) of tracks at a height of around 18,000 ft. (5,485m). The clearest ones showed a huge foot, roughly 8 in. (20cm) by 13 in. (33cm), with four toes.

Giants and shape shifters

Being able to change shape gives a being a lot of power. Shape shifters can sneak up on people without being recognized and escape unnoticed after performing some dastardly deed. Some shape shifters assume the shape and characteristics of another creature—for example, if they turn into a cat, they might take on a cat's hunting and tracking skills. Others can change only their size, becoming tiny or gigantic at will. Whether or not they can change shape, giants are also powerful figures in myths.

Forest guardian
In Mesopotamian mythology, Humbaba was a giant with a human body, lion's paws, and a face made of coiled intestines. Humbaba guarded the Cedar Forest until he was killed by the hero Gilgamesh and the wild man Enkidu.

Enormous creatures

Owing to their huge size, most giants had great strength and stamina. Mountains were sometimes believed to have been built by giants; in other cultures, they were explained as being the bodies of sleeping giants. Greek myths tell of the Cyclopes, a race of one-eyed giants. The first Cyclopes were blacksmiths who forged thunderbolts for Zeus. Their descendants became shepherds on the Italian island of Sicily. The hero Odysseus was trapped by one of these Cyclopes, a giant named Polyphemus.

Tricking the giant
When Polyphemus was asleep, Odysseus blinded him with a sharp stick taken from a fire. The next morning, Odysseus and his men escaped from Polyphemus's cave by clinging onto the bellies of the giant's sheep as they were let out to graze.

Scandinavian giants

According to Norse myths, trolls were huge, ugly creatures that lived in caves and burrows. They were very strong and had terrible tempers. They came out at night to lurk in the shadows and attack people, but if they were still out at sunrise, the sunlight turned them to stone.

Changing shape

The Algonquin people believed that a man-eating shape shifter called the Wendigo roamed the forests of southern Canada. It usually took the form of a giant man or a gray wolf. The Wendigo traveled in blizzards, using the weather as a cloak so that it could sneak up on its victims. Its scream paralyzed people with fear, and they could not run away.

Japanese giant

Shuten Doji was a terrible *oni* (ogre) who lured young girls to its mountain lair and ate them or kept them prisoner. The hero Minamoto no Yorimitsu and his friends decided to kill the *oni*. Disguised as monks, they crept up on it and got it drunk. Then Yorimitsu cut off Shuten Doji's head.

Werewolves

In popular stories, werewolves were the ultimate shape shifters. They looked human for most of the month and then revealed their true natures during the full moon, when they took the form of wolves. This type of transformation is called lycanthropy. Just one bite from a werewolf turned its victim into a werewolf, too. Werewolves were very hard to kill. One way was to shoot them with a silver bullet. Another was to use a weapon blessed in a chapel devoted to Saint Hubert, the patron saint of hunters.

Changed into a beast

In Greek myths, King Lycaon was visited by the god Zeus, who had disguised himself as an ordinary traveler. Lycaon served his guest a meal of human flesh, and this made Zeus so furious that he turned Lycaon into a wolf. The king regained his human form only after ten years of not eating human flesh.

Howling at the moon

In their wolf form, werewolves had no control over their actions. They howled at the moon, ran on all fours, and tracked down unsuspecting victims such as people who were out walking at night. They also used their paws to dig up fresh graves in order to get to the bodies buried inside.

A 12th-century Breton tale

Baron Bisclavret was a werewolf who became trapped in his wolf form after his wife hid his clothes. The gentle wolf was later adopted by the king of Brittany, France. When his wife appeared at court, Bisclavret bit off her nose, and her wicked deception came to light at last.

The beast of Gévaudan

During the 1760s, Gévaudan (present-day Lozère), France, was terrorized by a huge wolflike beast. It killed 88 people. The creature was never officially identified, but the attacks stopped after several large wolves in the area were shot.

The beast of Morbach

Tales about werewolves have continued to modern times. The little town of Wittlich, Germany, is said to be the last place where a werewolf was killed. It has a shrine in which a candle always burns. People said that if the candle ever went out, werewolves would return. In 1988, security staff on their way to work at a munitions base in Morbach, near Wittlich, noticed that the candle had gone out. Later that night, sirens went off at the base and the security men found a 26-ft. (8-m)-tall doglike beast preparing to jump over the fence. It fled before they could capture it. The candle at the Wittlich shrine was relit, and the creature has not been seen since.

Guardians of the underworld

People have always believed in gods and other worlds. Gateways between worlds were often protected by impressive guardians who were sometimes gods and sometimes incredible animals. Cerberus was possibly the most frightening. Belonging to Hades, the Greek god of death, Cerberus was a three-headed dog. In some stories it had a dragon's tail and snakes growing from its back. Cerberus guarded the gates to the underworld and greeted the dead. People were sometimes buried with three honey cakes. The belief was that they would give one to each of Cerberus's heads in order to keep its terrible jaws busy.

The last labor of Hercules

In penance for a fit of madness, Hercules had to carry out 12 tasks, or labors. The last was to bring the hound Cerberus out of the underworld. First, Hercules asked permission from Hades and Persephone, the king and queen of the underworld. Once that had been granted, he used his superhuman strength to drag Cerberus up into the daylight. At the same time, he rescued his cousin, the hero Theseus.

Poisonous plant

Cerberus resisted being dragged from its home and fought back as Hercules hauled it along. As the dog struggled and snapped, saliva flew from its three mouths. Wherever the saliva landed, a poisonous plant called aconite, or wolfsbane, sprang up.

Battle with the beast

During the final battle at the end of the world—according to Norse mythology—a monstrous dog named Garm will break loose and fight to the death with Tyr, the god of courage and honor. Both Tyr and Garm will lose their lives in the battle.

Guard dogs

The dog Garm guarded Helheim, the Norse land of the dead, and stopped the dead from returning to the world of the living. Garm was horrifying to look at, and blood dripped from its jaws. Dogs also appear in relation to the afterworld in Hindu teachings. The god Yama, known as the first being to die, guided the dead to the next world with the help of his two hounds, Syama the black and Sabala the spotted. Although they were fierce, these dogs could be calmed by gifts of raw meat.

The Egyptian underworld

In ancient Egyptian mythology, the underworld was guarded by the goddess Ammit, who had the head of a crocodile, the front legs of a lion, and the hindquarters of a hippo. Ammit waited near the scales of justice, upon which a dead person's heart was weighed. If the heart outweighed a feather, it was heavy with sin. The dead person was turned away, and Ammit ate the heart.

CREATURES OF THE WATER

Throughout history, sailors have feared violent storms at sea—with good reason. Small ships can be swallowed easily by waves or smashed against rocks. Many people believed that praying to the gods who controlled the storms would keep them safe. However, a whole range of other creatures were connected to disasters at sea, from mermaids and Sirens to terrifying sea serpents. Fresh water could be just as dangerous, housing terrible lake monsters or malicious spirits.

Strange sounds

Sirens were said to lure sailors to their deaths with their singing. The wind was probably responsible for many of the eerie sounds that sailors heard. Whistling through holes in rocks or echoing through caves, the wind can make a variety of sounds. The "singing" of whales and dolphins might also have sounded human to people who had never heard such a thing before.

Explaining the ocean

Natural phenomena, such as whirlpools, were also thought to be caused by supernatural beings. In Greek mythology, Charybdis was a sea nymph who kept flooding the land in order to extend the watery kingdom of her father, Poseidon, the sea god. Angry that she was taking so much land, Zeus turned Charybdis into a monster with an unquenchable thirst. Each day she sucked in huge amounts of water—and sometimes ships, too.

Deadly music

The Sirens were dangerous creatures who enchanted sailors with their singing. Usually depicted as great beauties who were half women, half fish, they were sometimes also shown with eagles' wings.

43

Mermaids and Sirens

According to folklore, mermaids live in a land of riches and splendor under the sea. They have fish tails but look like women from the waist up. Known for their beautiful singing voices, they are said to sing while sitting on rocks and combing their long hair. Like Sirens, mermaids' songs tempt passing sailors to bring their boats closer. Sailors often drown when their boats smash against the rocks, and the mermaids collect their souls, which they keep in cages in their underwater kingdom.

The fairy Melusine
In French and German fairy tales, Melusine had a woman's body, a serpent's tail, and, sometimes, wings. In one version of the story, Melusine looked like a normal woman every day but Saturday. In this depiction from 1500, her husband discovers her true nature.

Misunderstood?
Some people did not believe that mermaids were trying to harm sailors and shipwreck them on the rocks. They claimed that mermaids could see the future and that they sang to warn sailors when storms were on the way.

Siberian seal women

Many cultures tell tales of selkies, or seal women—seals that shed their skin and come ashore in human form. Seal women often fall in love with or even marry human men, but eventually the lure of the sea is too strong and they return to live as seals.

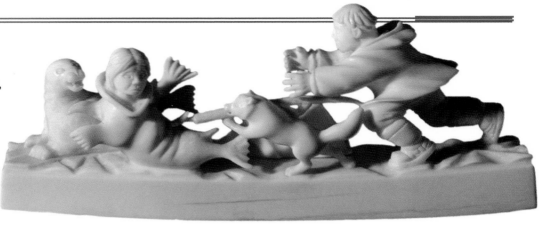

A Siren and her lyre

This 19th-century painting shows a Siren resting on a rock. When the Greek hero Odysseus had to sail past the Sirens, he made his men tie him to the mast so that he would not steer the ship into destruction. Then the sailors plugged their ears with wax. In this way, Odysseus heard the Sirens' music without putting the sailors' lives at risk.

Sirens

The Sirens of ancient Greek myths lived on a small uninhabited island off southern Italy. Many sailors lost their lives on the treacherous rocks that surrounded the island. This was blamed on the Sirens, whose songs promised knowledge of the past and the future. As they sailed near, the men saw that the rocks were scattered with the bones of the Sirens' previous victims, but by then it was too late for them to save themselves. In other versions of the story, the sailors died of starvation because they were so enchanted by the songs that they even forgot to eat.

Sea serpents

Throughout history, there have been tales of serpents rising up out of the ocean and attacking ships. The Greek writer Aristotle reported how local fishermen saw sea creatures that were like "beams of wood." Sea serpents are often described as having many humps down their backs. In other accounts, the monsters have long crocodilian heads or fins that resemble a dragon's wings.

Strange sightings

There are more than 1,200 written accounts of people seeing sea serpents. Sometimes a serpent might have been observed for hours by several witnesses. Most sightings date back to the days before photography, however, and there is no evidence that sea serpents actually exist.

A real monster?

In 1977, fishermen onboard the *Zuyo Maru* netted a huge snakelike creature off the coast of New Zealand (left). Before they threw it back into the water, the crew took pictures and tissue samples. So far, no one has been able to identify the creature.

Spotted close to shore

Unexplained sightings are not restricted to the open ocean. In 1985, twin brothers Robert and William Clark spotted a long, dark, snakelike creature chasing seals in San Francisco Bay, California. It moved by rolling its body into coils and wiggling up and down, and it had fins along its sides that acted like stabilizers.

Mythical sea serpent

In Norse myths, the god Odin banished the world serpent, Jörmungandr, to the seas. The beast grew so enormous that his body encircled the planet. Thor, the god of thunder, once caught the serpent and almost killed him with his hammer. At the end of the world, according to legends, Thor and Jörmungandr will battle each other, as shown here—and both will die.

Maori monster

This carved Maori post shows the heroic navigator Kupe holding up his paddle as a sign of victory. He has just defeated Te Wheke-a-Muturangi, a monstrous mythical octopus.

Dangerous bounty

When the kraken rose up from the depths, it brought many fish to the surface. This occurrence caused fishermen to risk their lives trying to catch the fish, in spite of the deadly suction created when the kraken sank back down.

Monsters of the deep

Serpents and sea snakes are not the only monsters that people have seen out at sea. Some sea monsters can be explained as real animals or weather phenomena. Others are harder to account for. Around the coasts of Norway, stories are told of a strange creature called the kraken that would emerge from the murky water. Although it posed no direct threat to fishermen, the kraken was deadly—when it sank back beneath the waves, it created a whirlpool that was powerful enough to suck a ship to its doom. Other monsters of the deep include the Bible's leviathan, a huge horned sea serpent that breathed fire so that the water all around it boiled.

Snatching sailors

Scylla was a six-headed sea monster from Greek mythology who used to grab sailors from passing ships and gobble them up. She shared the narrow strait of water where she lived with the whirlpool Charybdis (see page 43).

Grimm tales

The German brothers Grimm recorded the folktale of Queen Theodelinda, who was attacked by a sea monster. A passing nobleman rescued her, and she returned to her husband, King Agilulf. Theodelinda never told Agilulf about the attack, but later she gave birth to the sea monster's son. The boy was brought up as the king's own child, but he was evil through and through. Eventually, it became clear that the monstrous child had to be killed.

Death of the monster boy
King Agilulf and his knights fired arrows at the queen's evil son, but they could not kill him. The boy died only after his own mother shot him. Once the child was dead, Theodelinda told Agilulf about the wicked sea monster, and the king killed the monster at last.

Lake monsters

Deep lakes are the homes of many legendary beasts. Myths about Loch Ness, Scotland, date back to as early as A.D. 565, when Saint Columba saw a monster there. He shouted and made the sign of the cross, and the monster fled. Since then, more than 1,000 people claim to have seen "Nessie." Many have tried to explain the monster's presence. Some say that it is a plesiosaur, a marine reptile from the age of dinosaurs. Others believe that it could be a giant fish or a huge long-necked seal. Some people suggest that underwater volcanoes sometimes disrupt the surface of the loch, making it look as if something strange is swimming there.

What was Slimy Slim?
Between 1930 and 1945, around 30 people reported seeing a monster in Payette Lake in Idaho. Slimy Slim, also known as Sharlie, had a serpent's body, a long neck, and a flattened crocodilian head. The beast was never captured or identified.

Does the camera lie?
Taken in April 1934, this photograph of the Loch Ness monster was revealed to be a hoax in 1993. It actually shows a sculpted head attached to a toy submarine. Even so, thousands of people visit the loch each year, hoping to catch a glimpse of Nessie.

The Ogopogo

Lake Okanagan is an extremely deep, large lake in British Columbia, Canada. It is said to be home to a huge monster called the Ogopogo or, in the language of the native Salish people, *N'ha-a-itk*. Also known as the "great beast in the lake" or "snake in the lake," the creature has a serpentlike body and an enormous head and eyes. It has often been sighted at twilight or during storms. Some observers claim to have seen three of these creatures swimming side by side.

Mystery monster
This old black-and-white postcard of Lake Okanagan seems to show the Ogopogo with its serpentine humps. Although the monster has been seen and photographed many times, scientists still do not know what it is.

Harmless beast
People who have seen the Ogopogo claim that it feeds on waterweeds and small fish—so, despite its fearsome appearance, it poses no threat to humans. Even so, people avoid the area around Squally Point, where the monster's cave is said to be located.

Water horses

Hippocampi—swimming horses that had the head and front legs of a horse but the tail of a fish or dolphin—appear in the mythology of many ancient seafaring peoples. The Greeks, for example, believed that *hippocampi* pulled the chariot of their sea god, Poseidon. Other water horses were less helpful. The Scottish kelpie, Icelandic *nykur*, and Scandinavian *neck* were all evil spirits that took the form of a horse in order to lure people to a watery end.

Scary apparitions

Kelpies, which were evil spirits in Celtic folklore, often appeared as ponies. They tempted someone to ride them and then headed for the water and drowned their rider. In this illustration from 1821, however, a kelpie has taken on a very different appearance and has risen up from the water to give someone a fright.

King of the waves

Poseidon, the Greek god of the sea and of horses, ruled from the ocean floor in a palace made from gemstones and coral. His chariot was pulled by powerful *hippocampi*. The waves parted ahead of Poseidon's golden chariot—and sea monsters paid tribute to him as he passed.

Breaking the ice

Tales of mysterious horses were common in Icelandic myths. The magical *nykur* looked a lot like a horse but had backward-facing ears and hooves. Like the kelpie, it enticed riders to climb onto its back and then galloped off into deep water and drowned them. During the winter, when the lakes and rivers had frozen over, people feared crossing the ice. They said that the cracking noise caused by the ice breaking was actually the *nykur* neighing.

Scared off by its name

A *nykur* usually appeared as a gray horse but could transform itself into anything. The only defense against a *nykur* was to say its name. At the sound of this, the *nykur* would rear up in a panic, gallop off, and disappear into the water.

Dangerous spirits

Aboriginal devil
The bunyip was a man-eater of Australian folklore that lived in freshwater lakes, rivers, and creeks. Its name meant "devil." The bunyip was said to have a bellowing roar that could strike fear into people for miles around.

Some mythical creatures hurt people accidentally, but others did it on purpose. Vengeful spirits often made their homes near fast-flowing rivers, deep pools, or lakes with unexpected currents. They lured unsuspecting travelers into the water and drowned them. Others made strange sounds from the water's edge and then captured any curious passersby. In parts of Eastern Europe, these spirits were said to belong to people who had been drowned themselves. In other stories, the water spirits were not harmful at all. Their dancing on the surface of the water was simply a warning that someone was going to drown.

Water demons

Sometimes the pranks played by water spirits were more mischief than menace. The *kappa* of Japanese folklore was a creature around the size of a ten-year-old child that lived in ponds and rivers and looked like a cross between a monkey and a frog. The *kappa* got its strength from the water that filled the strange hollow space on top of its head. If a passerby could trick the *kappa* into spilling the water, he or she would be able to escape unharmed. One way to do this was to bow to the *kappa*. It was such a polite creature that it could not resist bowing back—and spilling the water!

Mischief-maker

The Japanese *kappa* played seemingly harmless tricks, such as looking up ladies' kimonos or passing gas noisily as people walked by, but it could also eat children. The only food *kappas* liked more than children was cucumbers. Parents would throw a cucumber into the water before swimming or bathing with their children.

The *vodyanoi*

In Eastern Europe, people believed that spirits called *vodyanois* lived in ponds, lakes, and streams. Around the size of an overweight old man, the *vodyanoi* had huge webbed hands and was often covered with algae and slime. If any young girls drowned in the water, it took them as its brides.

Folklore of today

All around the world, people believe that animals hold special powers. They may bring good or bad luck or they may foretell what will happen in the future, from predicting a coming storm to what type of person someone might marry. Images of creatures that are lucky in folklore appear on protective talismans and charms.

Ants

Ants Known for their tireless energy, ants are seen as bringers of good fortune. An ants' nest could be a sign of prosperity or fertility. Indian folklore tells of giant gold-digging ants that are larger than foxes.

Badgers In Europe, badgers' teeth are considered lucky. In Japanese folklore, the badger is a trickster.

Bears In many cultures, bears are symbols of strength, courage, and war. Viking warriors called berserkers wore bearskins into battle.

Bees

Bees In European folklore, a swarm of bees is a sign of forthcoming wealth. In Christian symbolism, beehives represent busy communities of monks.

Birds Free-flying birds are often associated with the human soul. A bird flying into a room and then out again is an omen that someone in the building will die.

Bulls Usually associated with life and energy, bulls are a sign of death in northern Asian folklore.

Black cat

Cats Worshiped as cult animals by the ancient Egyptians, cats were later distrusted. The Japanese told of cats that took over women's bodies. In Europe, the black cat might be a witch in animal form or represent the devil.

Crocodiles and alligators Because they cry fake "tears" after eating their prey, crocodiles are symbols of hypocrisy. In China, however, they are celebrated as the inventors of songs.

Dugongs and manatees Sightings of these sea mammals might be the source of mermaid myths.

Eagles The ancient Greeks associated the eagle with Zeus, the king of the gods. This powerful bird of prey remains a symbol of strength, victory, divinity, and eternal life.

Elephants Charms in the shape of elephants are believed to give strength to the wearers. Hindus seeking success make offerings to the elephant-headed god, Ganesh.

Toads

Frogs and toads The amazing transformation from tadpole to frog becomes, in fairy tales, a change from frog to prince. Finding frogs outside a house is lucky, but one inside signals death. Toads are linked to witches and bring bad luck.

Goats Since ancient times, goats have been associated with fertility.

Horses Witches were said to steal horses as mounts in European folklore. The way to deter them was to braid a horse's tail with ribbons.

Horses

Kingfishers Noah is said to have sent a kingfisher from the ark after a dove did not return. It flew too close to the sun and scorched its feathers.

Kingfisher

Lions In ancient cultures, lions were symbols of divinity and royal power. They were wise, courageous, and fierce. Lions contribute features to many mythical beasts such as griffins.

Lizards In Irish folklore, licking a lizard gives a person healing powers. These reptiles are also said to be used by witches as an ingredient in spells. In African and Pacific myths, lizards are guardian ancestors.

Lizard

Magpies In European traditions, it is bad luck to see a solitary magpie, but the Chinese believe that the magpie brings good fortune. It is always bad luck to kill a magpie, and eating its brain is thought to cause insanity.

Mice White mice are thought to be witches' imps in disguise. Seeing one cross the floor or leave the house is an omen of death.

Nightjars In the United States, anyone hearing the first call of the nightjar (a bird) in the spring should make a wish, as it is likely to come true.

Owls In France, if a pregnant woman hears an owl hooting, it is a sign that the baby will be a girl.

Parrots In Chinese folktales, parrots snitch on unfaithful wives.

Owl

Poodles In Germany, if a black poodle visits the grave of a priest, it is a sign that the man lived a sinful life.

Rabbits and hares Carrying a rabbit's foot is said to be lucky. In England, it is good luck to say, "White rabbits," before anything else on the first day of the month. In African and Native American myths, the hare is a trickster figure. The stories of Brer Rabbit are taken from these traditions.

Rabbit

Rats Known for their survival instincts, rats are said to be able to predict the sinking of a ship.

Robins Some Christians believe that the robin's breast was splashed red by Christ's blood. A robin tapping at a window is an omen of death.

Sheep Black sheep symbolize knowing and willful wrongdoers.

Snake

Snakes These reptiles are seen as guardians. Hanging up a snakeskin protects a house from fires. Snakes are also symbols of deception and evil.

Storks The Greeks linked storks to their goddess of childbirth, and in Western folklore, the stork brings babies. It is unlucky to kill a stork.

Tortoise

Tortoises Associated with eternal life, tortoises are considered lucky in many cultures. They symbolize slow but sure progress.

Wasps Killing the first wasp of the summer is supposed to bring good luck and protect the killer from his or her enemies.

Real-life monsters

Throughout history, people have associated magical qualities with animals or parts of animals such as their teeth or toes. Creatures of myths may be able to breathe fire, regrow heads, or detect poison, but the natural world boasts many animals that are just as amazing and monstrous. In fact, many mythological beasts have features based on real animals.

Crocodile

Crocodiles Lying motionless in rivers, crocodiles are extremely well camouflaged—they look just like floating logs! They ambush antelope, cattle, and other animals that come to the river to drink. Crocodile teeth are good for seizing and killing prey but are useless for chewing. Crocodiles drag their catch under the water and tear off chunks of flesh, which they swallow whole.

Ant lions These insects hunt alone, digging a pit in soft dirt or sand and then hiding at the bottom. If an unlucky ant falls into the trap, the sloping sides crumble as it tries to escape. Ant lions suck out an ant's insides and then throw away the body.

Aye-ayes These cat-size primates take their name from the alarm cry given when local people see them. Aye-ayes are considered an omen of death and are often killed on sight. In fact, they are harmless bug eaters.

Chameleon

Chameleons With their gripping tails and scaly bodies, chameleons look like real monsters. They can even swivel their eyes in different directions! When a chameleon spots its insect prey, it shoots out its tongue. In the blink of an eye, the tongue sticks to the prey and springs back into the mouth. With such a clever hunting method, these lizards deserve their name, which means "earth lion."

Fisherman bats These mammals hunt fish in rivers and lakes in Central and South America. Like all bats, they make use of a technique called echolocation, using sound waves to locate their prey. From the sounds made by ripples in the water, they can figure out the precise position of a fish. They snatch up the fish in their strong feet and carry it away to eat.

Fisherman bat and baby

Aye-aye

Bird-eating spiders Also known as tarantulas, bird-eating spiders are the world's largest spiders. They creep up on their prey and bite it with their venomous fangs. Bird-eating spiders eat mostly insects, but they also catch and devour mice and young birds. Instead of chewing their prey, they spit digestive juices onto it until it dissolves and then slurp it up.

Bird-eating spider

Giant squids Possibly growing up to 59 ft. (18m) long (the length of two buses), giant squids are the world's second-largest invertebrates. They hunt at depths of up to 3,300 ft. (1,000m), and their huge dinner-plate-size eyes let in as much light as possible so that they can locate fish and other prey in the darkness. Tales are told of terrible battles between giant squids and their main predators, sperm whales.

Gila (say "hee-la") monsters
These spotty-skinned lizards live in the deserts of the southwestern United States and northern Mexico and have a venomous bite. Their preferred food is small rodents, but they also eat young birds and eggs. They can gain as much as one third of their body weight in a single meal, but they can also go for long periods without eating any food.

Gila monster

Harpy eagles Living in the tropical forests of Central and South America, harpy eagles prey on monkeys and sloths. Strong and agile fliers, these eagles glide above forest canopies, occasionally swooping down to snatch an unlucky victim from a tree. Like the Harpies of myths, these birds of prey are armed with terrible claws.

Hyenas Hunting in packs, hyenas are animals of nightmares. Targeting weak or young animals, these hunting dogs run at speeds of up to 37 mph (60km/h), tripping their prey and snapping at its legs with powerful, bone-crushing jaws. A pack can ambush and eat a zebra in just 15 minutes, leaving only the indigestible hooves and hair behind.

Komodo dragon

Komodo dragons Native to Indonesia, Komodo dragons are the largest flesh-eating lizards. They feed on carrion—the dead bodies of other animals—and can grow up to 10 ft. (3m) in length. Although Komodo dragons are not venomous, their mouths are so full of bacteria that their bites often kill. The wounds usually become infected, and the victims die of blood poisoning.

Great white shark

Great white sharks The ultimate killing machines, great whites are predatory sharks that attack seals, dolphins, fish, and, sometimes, people. Their mouths are packed with rows of triangular razor-sharp teeth that are up to 3 in. (7.5cm) long. Great whites can follow a trail to a wounded creature, as they can sniff out a drop of blood in 26 gal. (100L) of water. They ambush from below, repeatedly taking bites out of a victim until it dies of blood loss.

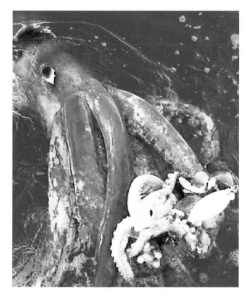

Giant squid

Portuguese men-of-war Like all jellyfish, Portuguese men-of-war ensnare their prey in their long, trailing tentacles, which are covered in stinging cells. If touched, these cells shoot out a poison that paralyzes prey so that the jellyfish can eat it.

Tasmanian devils These dog-size marsupials, or pouched mammals, are found on the Australian island of Tasmania. They let out a high-pitched scream when threatened or when defending food from other devils. Compared to their size, devils have the strongest bite of any mammal.

Tasmanian devil and babies

Thorny devils Belonging to the family of dragon lizards, Australia's thorny devils look frightening but are a threat only to ants. They may eat up to 2,000 ants in one meal, catching them one by one on their sticky tongues. They are also known as moloch lizards, after a Canaanite god to whom children were sacrificed.

Thorny devil

Glossary

abominable snowman Also known as the yeti, a large, apelike creature believed to live in the Himalayas of Asia.

afterworld The place where souls continue living after death; also known as the afterlife or underworld.

Ahuitzotl An Aztec monster that drowns and eats its victims.

Aztec A civilization that flourished in Mexico between the A.D. 1300s–1500s.

basilisk A monster with a reptilian body, wings, and a rooster's head.

Bigfoot Also known as Sasquatch, a large, apelike figure believed to live in remote forests in North America.

bogeymen Spiteful goblins said to kidnap children and frighten them into being good.

bogles and brownies Helpful household hobgoblins.

One of the Hydra's heads

bugaboos Frightening, shadowy goblins; also known as bugbears.

bunyips Man-eating creatures from Australian aboriginal myths.

centaurs Wild creatures of Greek myths that are half man, half horse.

Cerberus The three-headed dog that guards the Greek underworld.

Charybdis A Greek sea spirit often shown as a powerful whirlpool.

Chimera A fire-breathing monster of Greek myths with a lion's head, goat's body, and serpent's tail.

Chiron A wise, gentle centaur.

cockatrice Related to the basilisk, a four-legged rooster with a snakelike tail.

crocodilian Resembling a crocodile.

Cyclopes One-eyed Greek giants.

dragons Fire-breathing creatures with reptilian bodies and huge wings. Western dragons are malevolent; Eastern ones are a force for good.

fairies Humanlike beings, sometimes winged, that may grant wishes or bring good or bad luck.

feng-hwang A Chinese phoenix known for its faithfulness.

Fenoderee A fairy from the Isle of Man in the Irish Sea.

fertility The natural ability to produce crops or offspring.

firebird A mythical bird of Russian lore that brings good or bad fortune.

Furies Greek goddesses who punish people for their crimes.

Garm In Norse myths, the dog that guards Helheim, the land of the dead.

Garuda In Indian myths, a god that is half man, half bird.

giants Huge, mythical creatures that look similar to humans.

goblins Small, ugly, and humanlike beings that play nasty tricks.

Gorgons In Greek myths, three snake-haired sisters—Euryale, Stheno, and Medusa—who can turn people to stone by looking at them.

griffins Majestic beasts that are half lion, half eagle.

Harpies Three vengeful spirits from Greek mythology.

hippocampi In Greek myths, swimming horses with fishlike tails.

hobgoblins Mischievous fairies.

Humbaba A Mesopotamian giant killed by the hero Gilgamesh.

Hydra A nine-headed Greek beast that was killed by the hero Hercules.

immortality The ability to live forever and never die.

insignia A coat of arms.

Jörmungandr The "world serpent" of Norse mythology.

kappas Japanese water spirits.

kelpies Shape shifters of Celtic myths that often take the form of horses.

ki-lins Chinese unicorns.

kobolds German hobgoblins.

kraken A legendary sea monster that resembles a giant squid.

labyrinth A maze.

lair A monster's den or home.

lamassus In Mesopotamian myths, guardians that take the form of human-headed winged bulls or lions.

loch A Scottish lake or sea inlet.

Loch Ness monster Legendary serpent monster of Loch Ness, Scotland.

lutins French hobgoblins.

lycanthropy The act of changing into a wolf.

medieval Dating from the Middle Ages, roughly from A.D. 450 to 1450.

Medusa A Greek Gorgon killed by the hero Perseus.

Melusine In European lore, a freshwater spirit a lot like a mermaid.

mermaids Legendary sea beings that are half woman, half fish.

Minotaur A man-eating monster that was half bull, half man, killed by the Greek hero Theseus.

mortal Living for a period of time and then dying.

myrrh Scented, oily tree resin.

myth A traditional story, usually featuring gods, monsters, and heroes, that may explain natural phenomena.

nagas Snake gods of Indian myths.

nykur An Icelandic shape shifter that often appears as a gray horse.

Ogopogo A water demon that lives in Lake Okanagan, Canada.

ogres Man-eating giants of folklore.

omens Signs of something good or bad that will happen in the future.

onis Japanese ogres.

Pegasus A gentle winged horse from Greek mythology.

pharaohs The rulers of ancient Egypt.

phoenix A legendary bird that burns to death and then rises up from the ashes.

Polyphemus A Cyclops killed by the Greek hero Odysseus.

purushamrigas Indian Sphinxes.

pyramids Stone structures with square bases and sloping sides used in ancient Egypt as royal tombs and in Mexico and Central America as temples.

Poseidon and his *hippocampi*

roc A giant bird of Arabian myths.

sacrifice An offering made to please a god or monster.

Satyrs Forest-dwelling Greek gods that were half man, half goat.

Scylla A six-headed snakelike sea monster of Greek myths.

sea serpents Sea monsters with long, snakelike bodies.

selkies Seal women.

shape shifters Mythical creatures that can change into other forms.

shrines Sacred places dedicated to a particular god, being, or holy object.

Shuten Doji An *oni* killed by the hero Minamoto no Yorimitsu.

simurgh In Arabian mythology, an ancient and wise bird.

Sirens Greek enchantresses, half woman, half fish, who may have wings.

Sphinx In Egyptian myths, a creature with a lion's body and the head of a man, ram, or hawk. In Greek myths, a creature with a lion's body, a woman's head, and, sometimes, wings.

talismans Objects believed to have magic powers and to bring good luck.

Te Wheke-a-Muturangi A monster octopus of Maori myths.

thunderbird A Native American storm spirit and totem figure.

trolls In Norse myths, huge, ugly creatures that hunt humans at night.

unicorns Mythical white horses with a spiral horn on the forehead.

Valhalla In Norse myths, the great hall where heroes spend the afterlife.

Valkyries Norse goddesses who select warriors to live in Valhalla.

vampires Shape shifters that come out at night to feed on human blood.

vodyanois Eastern European water demons that drown people.

Wendigo A Native American giant that usually appears as a man or a wolf.

werewolves Shape shifters that change into the form of a wolf.

wyverns Also known as *vouivres*, small, dragonlike creatures with a serpent's body and eagle's wings.

yin and yang In Chinese beliefs, the two principles that make up everything. Yin is passive, dark, cold, feminine, and negative. Yang is active, light, warm, masculine, and positive.

Index

Further reading

Books
Fantasy Encyclopedia
  by Judy Allen, Kingfisher, 2005

Monsters: An Investigator's Guide to Magical Beings
  by John Michael Greer, Llewellyn Publications, 2001

Mythology (Eyewitness Companions) by Philip Wilkinson and Neil Philip, Dorling Kindersley, 2007

Mythology of the World
  by Neil Philip, Kingfisher, 2004

Myths and Legends
  by Anthony Horowitz, Kingfisher, 2007

Websites
An online encyclopedia of monsters:
www.monstropedia.org

A guide to famous mythological beasts:
http://monsters.monstrous.com/

A collection of animal myths and legends:
www.planetozkids.com/oban/legends.htm

An encyclopedia of mythology and folklore:
www.pantheon.org

A guide to the monsters and heroes of Greek myths:
www.mythweb.com

Acknowledgments

The publisher would like to thank the following illustrators for their contributions to this book:

b = bottom, *c* = center, *l* = left, *r* = right, *t* = top

Hemesh Alles (Maggie Mundy) 13*cr*; **Peter Dennis (Linda Rogers Assoc.)** 9*tr*, *b*; **Rebecca Hardy** 16*tl*; **Donald Harley (BL Kearley Ltd.)** 14, 23*br*, 29; **Nick Harris (Virgil Pomfret Agency)** 44–45; **Patricia Ludlow (Linden Artists)** 8, 50–51; **Nicki Palin** 6*cr*, 20, 40–41; **Bernard Robinson** 12*l*; **Planman Technologies (India) Pvt. Ltd.** 4–5, 6–7, 7*tl*, 10–11, 12–13, 15, 17, 18–19, 22–23, 24–25, 26–27, 28, 30–31, 32–33, 34–35, 36–37, 37*cr*, 38–39, 41*t*, 42–43, 46–47, 48–49, 49*br*, 52–53, 54–55

The publisher would like to thank the following for permission to reproduce their material:

b = bottom, *c* = center, *l* = left, *r* = right, *t* = top

Pages: **6***tl* Werner Forman Archive/Haiphong Museum, Vietnam; **9***cl* Bridgeman Art Library (BAL)/Lady Lever Art Gallery, National Museums Liverpool; **10***cl* BAL/Bibliothèque des Arts Decoratifs, Paris, France/Archives Charmet; **11***tc* BAL/Fred Jones Jr. Museum of Art, University of Oklahoma/Wentz-Matzene Collection, 1936; **11***br* Werner Forman Archive/Metropolitan Museum of Art, New York; **13***bl* The Art Archive/Biblioteca Augustea Perugia/Dagli Orti; **14***cr* Corbis/Araldo de Luca; **15***tr* AKG/Kassel, Staatliche Kunstsammlungen; **16***bl* Corbis/John Springer Collection; **21***tl* The Art Archive/Private Collection/Dagli Orti; **21***cr* Corbis/Tim Graham; **21***bl* Werner Forman Archive; **22***cl* Corbis/Elio Ciol; **23***tr* The Art Archive; **24***tr* Alamy/© INTERFOTO Pressebildagentur; **25***tr* AKG/Bibliothèque Nationale, Paris, France; **26***l* Corbis/Luca I. Tettoni; **26***b* BAL/Archives Charmet; **28***br* The Art Archive/Dagli Orti; **29***tl* The Art Archive/Musée du Louvre/Dagli Orti; **30***tl* Corbis/Christie's Images; **33***tr* BAL/Archives Charmet; **34***tr* Getty/Ernst Haas; **34***bl, bc, br* Topfoto/Fortean; **35***tr* Alamy/Mary Evans Picture Library; **36***tl* BAL/British Museum; **37***tl* Alamy/Mary Evans Picture Library; **37***bl* V&A Museum, London; **39***tl* Davison Art Center, Wesleyan University, Connecticut; **39***bl* BAL/Musée Nationale des Arts et Traditions Populaires; **41***br* The Art Archive/Egyptian Museum, Turin; **44***l* Alamy/Mary Evans Picture Library; **45***t* Bryan and Cherry Alexander/Arcticphoto; **45***c* BAL/Leeds Museums & Art Galleries; **47***tl* Yano Michihiko/www.gennet.org; **47***br* Mary Evans Picture Library; **48***tl* Kahuroa, New Zealand; **49***tl* AKG/Peter Connolly; **50***tr* Alamy/Joshua Roper; **50***cl* Getty Hulton; **51***tr* Topfoto/Fortean; **52***c* Alamy/Mary Evans Picture Library; **54***c* The Art Archive/Museum für Völkerkunde Vienna/Dagli Orti; **55***tl* Werner Forman Archive/Private Collection; **56***tl* Corbis/Michael & Patricia Fogden; **56***tr* Getty/Pure Images; **58***tr* Frank Lane Picture Agency/Winfrid Wisniewski; **58***cl* Photolibrary/David Haring; **58***cb* Natural History Picture Agency/Martin Harvey; **59***tc* Natural History Picture Agency/Daniel Heuclin; **59***cl* Corbis/DLILLC; **59***cr* Natural History Picture Agency/Dave Watts; **59***bl* PA Photos/Ap/Koji Sasahara; **59***bc* Frank Lane Picture Agency/Minden Pictures; **59***br* Frank Lane Picture Agency/Minden Pictures